the anatomy
of an arsonist.

the anatomy of an arsonist.
Copyright © 2020 by rose devika.

ISBN: Soft Cover – 978-1-64318-060-1

Imperium Publishing
1097 N. 400th Rd
Baldwin City, KS, 66006

www.imperiumpublishing.com

the anatomy
of an arsonist.

poems by
rose devika.

IMPERIUM PUBLISHING
CREATE YOUR STORY

for sebastian.

III. oxygen and the lungs.

rose devika.

I.
combustible material
&
the nervous system.

home.

i have lived in two countries, three states, eight cities,
four houses, a dorm room, two apartments,
the back of my car,
and more living rooms than i can count.
i am far too restless,
to stay stagnant.
it is true, that i am most often build of fight or flight,
the former first,
the latter immediately after.
i have spent most of my life searching
for something to call home,
but am terrified of finding a house with a heartbeat,
a metronome
steady enough to keep the fault lines,
from splitting the tremor of ground beneath me.
it is far easier to phoenix,
it is far easier to burn every bridge i have built,
to rebuild from the ashes,
again and again.

soldier.

i walk into a restaurant somewhere in new york city.
flash my teeth white,
like blood diamonds,
like something cut,
and clear,
and stolen.
i shake hands with the man four times my age,
with lines that trace across his face
like highways on a dusty map,
and a tongue that sputters,
stalls,
stutters,
like it has run all out of gasoline,
all out of drive.
and i hope his eyes will skid across my cold shoulder,
sharpen it into blade,
i hope he will say something fast enough
for me to hit the brakes, to break open
my marble expression.
i hope for hazard.
for headlights.
for bite.
for quick trigger, pull,
click.

if happiness is a warm gun,
i want to be fevered metal,
burning and begging for the bullet of rage,

and so i stay,
hoping he will invite me back to some motel room,
with starched white sheets he can unwrap me from
like a body bag.
i hope to be the flag.

mourning for morning at half mast,
a mask of rag doll and still stature,
stone statue and plastic,
eyes, closing caskets.

i hope my body elastic enough
to snap into flinch, into swing,
into sing these noose notes.
let youth hang
like a crucified melody.
call this holy.

hold me in your battered fists,
build your body of styrofoam,
and let me be the wrecking ball

rose devika.

but jesus christ.
i still cannot break loud enough
for the truth to release its hostages.

across the table,
i stare down the lack of life in his eyes.
wish them empty sockets,
wish them electric enough to shock
this apathy into anger,
wish for my backbone to bend
from a question mark into a fist,
into a fight,
so i can finally write this war out of me.

instead, he tells me that when he was young
and was drafted for the vietnam war,
he almost bought a train ticket to canada
because he has never been a soldier.
tells me the older he gets,
the more loneliness loads its gun.
says he has swallowed all of his bullets.
starts shooting off his mouth.

becomes the little boy being drafted again.

and suddenly we are both so small
and so much the same.
and suddenly, every creased highway becomes a lifeline,
my spine uncurling into a tightrope
i can string across the table,
and back to hope.

he pays with an envelope of cash,
and a book of poetry.
tells me,
not everyone is the battle i make them out to be.

months later,
when I can no longer afford to live in new york
he pays for my train ticket to canada.

tells me i do not always have to be a soldier.
tells me the war will be over
soon
enough.

she, a storm.

at first,
the air is nothing but a warm bath,
and i stand barefoot on the balcony,
wild-eyed,
anticipating all that will fall,
hungry for the chaos,
shifting on the horizon.

everything far too silent,
until it spills across that ledge of sky,
becomes summer storm
tearing through all that can be torn.

until rain rages in slanted crescendos,
until thunder becomes hammer,
cracking the concrete.

all that is malleable
cowering in tremor,
loosening its grip on faith,
twisting
into dissonance and turmoil.

even the trees hunch their shoulders,
tense up each limb,
bend their backs until the crack of lightning

splits them into perfect halves.

destruction and all its symmetry,
destruction and all its terror,
all its ruthless beauty.

the body of the storm,
the way she builds best under pressure.

her windpipes,
her breathless.

her dare the danger,
her try to tie me into submission.

how quickly she
comes.

rose devika.

how quickly she settles,
becomes again, restless,

leaves without a word.

returns relentlessly,
intensity, heat, and heartbeat,

all that unbridled instability,

how willingly
we both lose control.

a conversation in choreography.

highway 1 has scoliosis,
a curved question mark of coastline,
a spinal chord,
bent and tuned to the pacific blues,
every cliff rising
in just the right pitch.

so i named my car smith.
because i swear,
every note of 'louder than bombs'
could have been written to nothing
but the song of curved highway,
car engine,
arching feet,

and you.
standing on the passenger seat,
reaching for that sky,
an open wound,
your ribcage already so bruised,
from all the times you asked me
to put my hand over your heart,
to feel how goddamn hard it was beating,

your way of keeping time.

and we never really had time.

but we were still the sweetest conversation in choreography.
cartography,
mapping out the fastest route to the root
of full fucking honesty,

astronomy had nothing on our study of stars,
how to stitch them into streetlamps,
call it our spotlight.
that empty audience of oil rigs,
bowing,
to our first and final act.

your fingertips against the small of my back,
miming train track out of vertebrae,
sometimes, the only way to communicate
is through movement.

and we were so fluent in sway,
in three-step, no stumble,
neither of us clumsy,
but still so quick to trip
in love.

rose devika.

lawless, loose-lipped, long-gone lover,

do you remember that gospel of a waltz,
all stratosphere, soft snare, and saxophone?

do you remember the first car ride home,
when you fell asleep
with your head resting against my collarbone?

i spent two weeks sanding down
the right of my shoulder blade,
just in case you got tired again,
because i wanted to give you nothing
but my soft side to lean on.

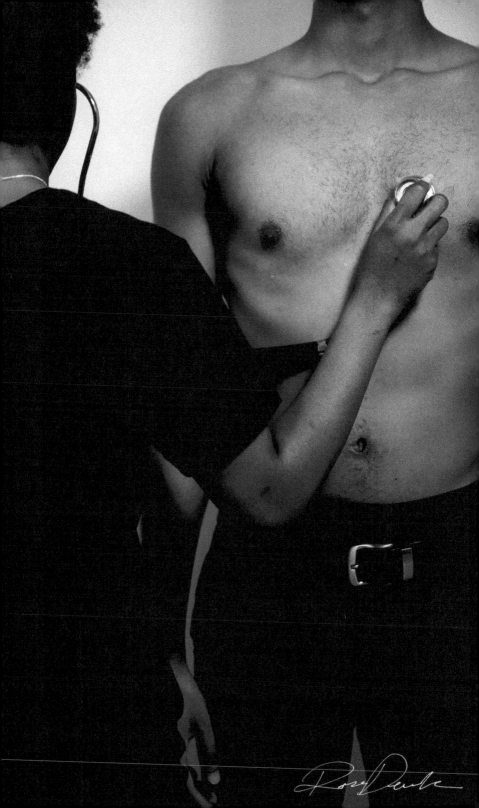

i could.

i could leave her

for someone more flammable.
for a body more bridge to burn.

all the pretty girls and boys in bars,
lost or lonely,
looking for arson and unholy.

with chiseled cheekbones
and feather teeth.
more air than body,
skin,
so easily turned canvas.

i could paint their spines
into highways,
pull my lips over to the shoulder,
show them the way my eyes light up
both labyrinths
and exit signs.

i could self-destruct,
become the catalyst,
for the chaos

those looking for self-destruction
are looking for.

when finished,
i could light their cigarettes,

turn my teeth mirror,
smile them into believing
i am what they need.

i could manipulate my every move,
power trip over my own guilt trip,

i could rely on them,
lie to them,
lie with them.
empty them.

i could carve out convictions,
convince myself
that this,
this is what happiness must feel like.

love,
just a game to play,

love,
check mate,

or,
i could learn what it means to stay.

if you've been, you know.

new york is the love letter
you don't want to write,
but do anyway.

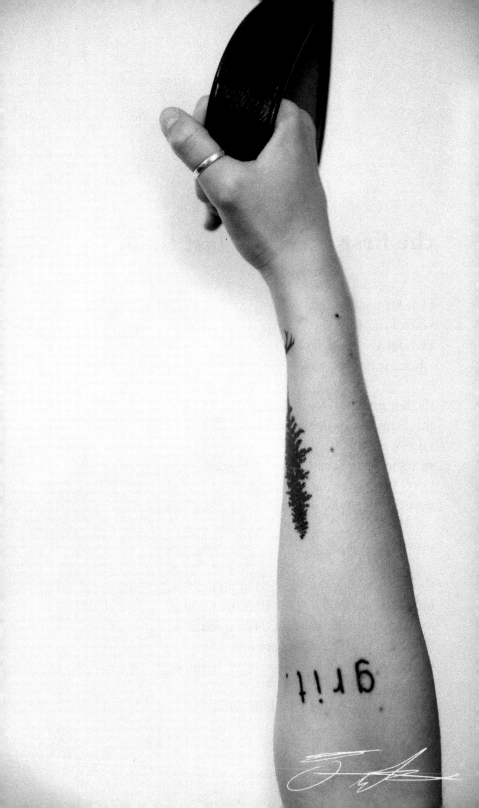

the first time, the last time.

i left for the first time
when i was fourteen,
i left for the last time
when i was eighteen.

the last time my older brother
threw me across the room,
i drove eight hours,
straight down pacific coast highway.
never turned on the headlights,
never checked the rearview.

i rarely look back.

the last time my mother tried to pull
my little brother down the stairs by his hair
i wrapped my hands around her throat,
the first time i was strong enough,
to lay my tough against the soft of her neck,

she hasn't laid a finger on him since.

the last time i saw my father (biologically),
(and for the first time, it really was the last),
he swung at me in the parking lot behind my apartment,

and i swung back.

those are the only two times
i have let the blood on their hands become mine.

the last time i saw my little brother,
i told him what our brother (biologically)
had done to me for seven years.

the fifteen years it took me to tell him,
i couldn't stop apologizing,
for not protecting him from the truth this time.

he wrapped his arms around my shoulders,
i told him that he shouldn't have to comfort me,
he told me that i have always been there,
and he will be, too,
that that is what sisters and brothers
are meant to do.

rose devika.

he, always the softest, the wisest
of us all.

told me he trusted me
more than anyone in this world.

i will never in my life
forget those words.

i will never question,
what love feels like.

you are so loved.

the moon looks like pale origami tonight,
folded into bruised sky,
the familiarity of your footsteps,
the way they move almost soundlessly,
pause,
the way you crack open my bedroom door.

your windpipes,
the softest wind chimes,
whispering my name
to see if i am still awake.

i have slept through a fire alarm,
a rock concert,
and a wedding.

but it is muscle memory,
to wake up
the moment i hear even the slightest
fragment of fear in your voice.
you, far too young
to sleep so restlessly,
i, far too old to
nightmare so frequently.

your baby hairs curl around cowlick,
your head curls into my shoulder,
asleep so quickly.

baby brother,
you are the most definite definition
of love
i have ever known.

and i swear,
i will spend every moment of this life
teaching you love,
teaching you grace,
teaching you trust.

cold cardiac.

verse 1:
the cruelest month,
november's touch,
those belt buckle teeth,
weak knees,
don't you dare try to speak.

mama's been lying
off-pitch,
but somehow in tune,
floodgates roll open,
heartbreak monsoon.

chorus:
the wind it bites but i bite back,
icicle arteries thaw,
cold cardiac,
i won't go back.

our house was built on a fault line
and i still shake,
even after all these miles,
so i won't, no i won't go back.

verse 2:
i learned love in atrophy,

slowly coil this body,
into something weak.

resilience itself
terrifies me,
but we march on,
always off-beat.

chorus:
the wind it bites but i bite back,
icicle arteries thaw,
cold cardiac,
i won't go back.

our house was built on a fault line
and i still shake,
even after all these miles,
so i won't, no i won't go back.

rose devika.

angel.

monika,
the day you tried to return your life,
i prayed to every god i have never known.
none of them called back.

i found only the residue of resilience,
cobwebs cluttering all of your baggage,
the breath you couldn't catch,
the train of thought,
you let run rampage and off the rails,
its wreckage a collision of metal and fire.

to live in a body
you want to scratch and claw your way out of,
to become a howling beast,
a white horse, pawing the ground into grave,
beating the life that built you black and blue,
all of that wild in you.
the bloodstream, boiling.

i cracked open everything
i thought i knew about grief.
turned my tongue into the smooth of a pebble,
every word,
a desperate stone skipping,

anything to find its way to your shore,
a plea that i could use echolocation,
just to hear your pulse shiver back.

it took them three days to tell me
whether you were still alive or not.

every clock in my house stopped ticking
and started talking.
told time in slurred click,
the slowest motion i have ever moved through.

angel,
thank god you were desperate enough to die.
if it meant learning
you were far more desperate to live.

we have never assured each other of anything
we couldn't be certain of.
but we have said we will pull each other out
of the deep end, anytime.

and we always have,
and we always will.

nightmare.

verse 1:
talk me through the fever nightmare,
it's too loud in my head
the voices called again last night,
they taught me fear,
then left.

wrapped in twilight,
twisted sheets,
tight like a body bag,
i'll trade my life for some sleep,
raise my last white flag.

chorus:
restless electric hands,
i'm starting a war,
haunted history,
i've seen it all before.

do you have some anesthesia?
gotta give myself amnesia,
i need ya,
the ghosts are calling for me.

verse 2:
silent soldier,

i've grown older,
but in fear i'm a child
i sing myself to sleep some nights,
on others i just hide.

conversations rise in volume,
i have fought this fight,
they keep begging me
to listen,
say i can't love right.

chorus:
restless electric hands,
i'm starting a war,
haunted history,
i've seen it all before.

do you have some anesthesia?
gotta give myself amnesia,
i need ya,
the ghosts are calling for me.

verse 3:
watch myself step,
then fall,
from the eighteenth floor,

rose devika.

windows barricaded shut,
i don't know what's real anymore.

chorus:
restless electric hands,
i'm starting a war,
haunted history,
i've seen it all before.

do you have some anesthesia?
gotta give myself amnesia,
i need ya,
the ghosts are calling,
they're calling,
they're calling
for me.

rose devika.

forest fire.

heat rises.
and so do i,
for the first time.

90% of all wildfires are started by humans.
and all the untamed,
all that hungers to be set free,
spreads through every inch of this body of water.

it has finally reached boiling temperature,
the toil and twist of limbs,
i am the arsonist today,
the match, striking
for the first and last time.

i have never known
how resilient i am
until this very moment.

i become crown fire,
you, still the coward
you have always been,
buckle and cave in,
give up as easily
as you have on everything.

rose devika.

II.
heat
&
homeostasis.

open road, open grave.

somewhere
between the 55 north and the 91 east,
you write down our location,
directions,
the destination.

on the next page,

his eulogy.

somewhere between the 91 east and the 215 south,
you tune your acoustic heartstrings,
then snap them.

ask god
if he is still the conductor of this world,
nothing but a war-torn orchestra.

somewhere between the 60 east and the california 242,
your clavicle cracks concave,
hollow,
harrowed.

so we lean into grief,
its arms wrapped around us

like electric yellow tape,

death rarely offers a fire escape.
only open road,
only open grave.

we watch the sky split open
baptized in bruises.
a sinking soliloquy,
the softest sunset.

rose devika.

and in this moment
absolutely everything
and nothing at all
feels worthy of the word holy.

somewhere between west lincoln and a tiny town,
your eyes are the brightest blue
they have ever been
striking and unflinching

and i think we love each other
more right now,
than we ever have,

because life has not been kind
to either of us, lately

but we are still so fucking lucky
to live every moment
we have left to live.

rose devika.

hands and what they carry.

i have never studied hands the way i studied his.
memorizing every movement.

and though i often read facial expressions,
they are excruciatingly limited to the present,
most of us, far too aware of our own presence,
far too easy to feature our best features.

we carry the entirety of our history in our hands.
it can be read in even the most subtle light.

his hands were nearly twice the size of mine,
built to build or destroy,
the thumb of dominant hand alone,
pressed against neck,
would be enough to take my last in-breath,
carve lungs into collapse,
one last act of unwilling submission.

there is a reason i stayed so long.

his trigger finger,
what it was capable of.

his hands, the hands of my brother

handing me the mirror
so i could see myself compliant,
silent,
just as small as i used to be.

i traced across the circles and ridges in my fingertips,
the annual growth rings of a tree,
could almost see them moving in reverse.

we carry the entirety of our history in our hands.

fingers are filled with nerve endings,
his nerves always frayed and frustrated,
rage reigning,
fists clenched,
white knuckled,
muscle memory,
tensed tendons,
tying my wrists into rope burn.

his mood swung,
so did his hands,
he never hit me,

just got close enough,

rose devika.

to let my inner child win custody, again,
fear let himself right back in
not a fighting chance of evicting him.

we carry the entirety of our history in our hands.

and mine often tremor, they always have,
shake like the branches on a family tree,
the one i have fallen so far from,
so willingly.

we were both taught to use our hands as weapons,
to target the achilles heel,
we both know how to find the words that cut
straight to the bone,
that cannot be forgiven.

so hand me your sharpest knife,
the one that will slice all that you are
back to broken boy,
i will lay it down,
leave it to rust in the rain.

and that is the difference between us.
you would never do the same.

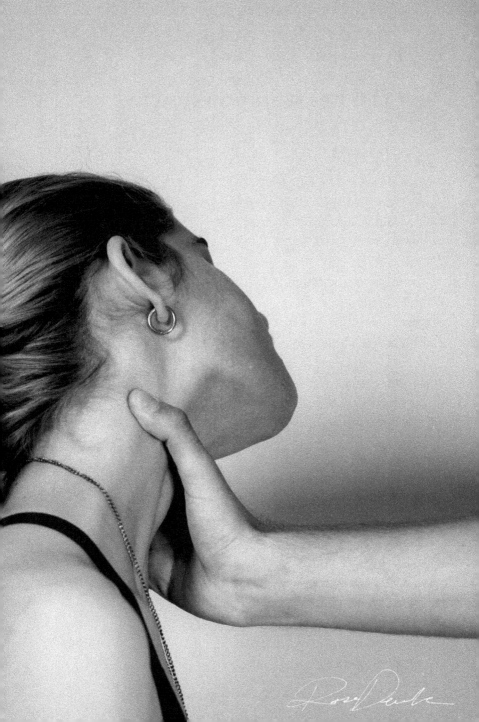

rose devika.

let the beast in you howl.

verse 1:
so you want to be king,
have everybody kneel at your feet,
kiss your knuckles,
kiss your ring.

i'm known to be tough,
make you crawl to me,
crave defeat,
i say when it's enough.

chorus:
power trip, tripwire, misfire,
hold me down,
wage war,
i win this round.

recklessly, ruthlessly ruin me,
i stand my ground,
wage war,
let the beast in you howl.

verse 2:
so you want to be known,
have everybody say your name,
worth for fame,

this, your lonely throne.

just know i am cruel
you still submit to me,
aim to please
add fire to the fuel.

chorus:
power trip, tripwire, misfire,
hold me down,
wage war,
i win this round.

recklessly, ruthlessly ruin me,
i stand my ground,
wage war,
let the beast in you howl.

rose devika.

mania, in red.

the ambulance screeches around the corner,
far too familiar,
a metallic flash of red,
a siren tuned to match hysteria in pitch.
a wailing anthem.

skyscrapers protrude like shrapnel
stuck in flesh,
unflinching.

movement,
motion,
mania.

memory lane is riddled with traffic.

paper boats.

my mother is like mother earth.
carries nature's curse under her skin,
her temper, a tempest
that never lets her rest.

even at her best,
i can never find the forecast,
see it only in the aftermath,
when her pulse is already ebbing and flowing,
a suicidal, tidal wave.

the bloodstream,
still echoing that scream of grief,
and its unwillingness to surrender.
i remember now,
how many times i have not spoken
because i don't want to be the cause
of her breaking open.
because i don't want to kickstart more dark into her life,
because her life
has been absent of light for long enough already.
but if i could, i would tell her that

one,
when i was young i wore my heart on my sleeve,

every time you would leave,
every time you would say we'd be better off without you,
every time you wanted to find the weather vein of your wrist,
every time you would insist
you were never coming back,
my words would panic attack,
stutter, like a broken record on repeat,
don't leave, don't leave, don't leave,
i still need you,

two,
i'm sorry that i once said that you are just like your mother,
i know it isn't your fault that you sometimes carry her touch
in your fingertips,
that your hand slips, hits, throws,
i know sometimes, you just need to anchor your anger
into something tangible.
an eye for an eye in the eye of your storm,
eyelids open,
we both mourn what we keep meaning to see,
but we don't see

three,
i don't wear my heart on my sleeve much anymore, but

rose devika.

four,
i am not apathetic, i am not indifferent.
it's just the consistent collateral damage,
has left my heart a monument,
that does not want to remember its own history,
so i have never given you my honesty,
because honestly,
these words would fall like a guillotine,
clamp onto your neck like teeth that time has made sharp,
and I don't want to leave bite marks like that.

five,
stay alive,

six,
you have to live,

because seven,
i believe only in the absence of heaven, and

eight,
i know how much weight you carry,

i know sometimes you just want the clocks to stop.
i know you get so caught in your own storm,
that you do not see the casualty you casually make,

of everything you cannot fight through,
and i know this, because i am just like you.
we both search every entrance for an exit sign, but

nine,
i hope you find a way to love this life.
in spite of all the light that doesn't shine through,
i hope you find a way to turn your heartstrings
into kite strings,
so that gravity does not pull you down so often.

for now, i will soften my words.
because i know how far you bend,
to give us the life you never got.
you taught me how badly I want to live,
taught me to give each out breath an anthem,
taught me to never hold the truth for ransom.

i have learned to turn suicide notes into paper boats
and sink them.

have learned to find forgiveness through a pen,

because ten,
we are both
still alive.

rose devika.

the car says crash.

the nurse lists all the risks,
says iv,
says ct scan,
says sometimes these things are lifelong.
says head trauma,
says specialist,

deep breath.

says bloodwork,
says medic,
says run a few tests,

deep breath.

says walk a straight line,
tiptoe like you are on a tightrope,
says stethoscope,
says off-beat heartbeat,
says follow the rhythm of my finger,
says bring her upstairs,
don't be scared.
says imaging,
says interesting,
says rate your pain on a scale from 1 to 10,
are you claustrophobic?

stay stoic,
stay rigid,
stay still,

deep breath.

the mri machine says swallow the scream,
says swallow you whole,
says imagine you are jonah,
the belly of the beast all teeth and tighten,
the stomach lining, metal and magnetic,

deep breath.

says watch me whir into the nape of your neck,
pound into your backbone,
until you are more drum than human,
less music and more sound,
says loud, loud, loud,
says wait for the results,
quick pulse,
quick pills,
peel the pillow from your head,
no rest yet,

deep breath.

rose devika.

the neurologist says gabapentin,
says beta blocker,
says botox injections,
says just a few more questions,
says 20 needles to the skull, neck, and shoulders,
says you warrior, you soldier,
says someone hold her
still.
3, 2, 1, inject,

deep breath.

just a temporary paralysis,
being expressionless only a side effect.

the psychiatrist says amitriptyline,
says depakote,
says xanax,
says panic,
says prozac.

the stranger says have you tried this,
and this,
and this quick fix.

the therapist says have you tried tapping,

my friend says have you tried laughing
it off.

the pain specialist says have you tried opioids,
an epidural, surgery.
the healer says have you tried mercy.
(then says he can see my atoms just like lasers,
says, just like the lightsabers in star wars).
the cardiologist says have you tried an echocardiogram,
a holter monitor,
a stress test,

deep breath.

the car says crash.
but i don't listen.

because my hope is my birthright,
because i was raised to fight for this life,
because my breath is still bending
across the shore of my chest,
because yes,
this has been the hardest year i have ever lived.
because my mama can't afford it,
but finds a way anyway,
because I keep capsizing,

rose devika.

treading water but surviving.
i keep surviving.

and though it doesn't get better tomorrow,
the way tomorrow always says it will,
i am still here.
still waiting for that promise of tomorrow,

knowing it will come,
and when it does,
my happiness will be the loudest thing
you have ever heard.

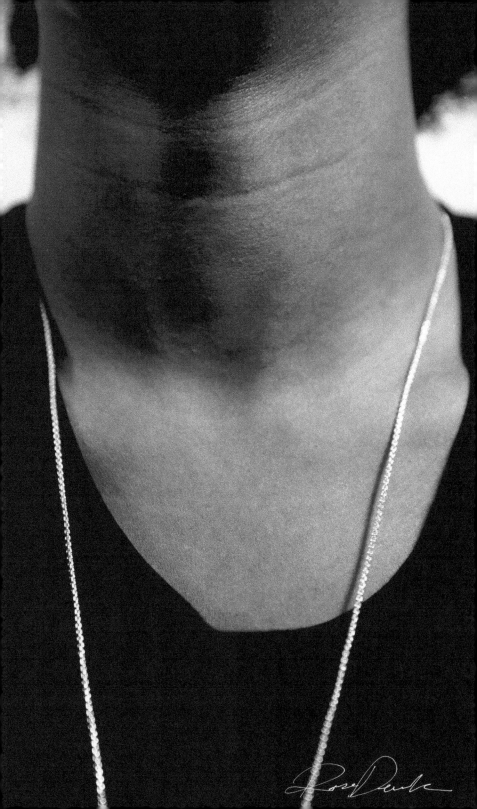

let me be someone new.

verse 1:
everything's been gray lately,
visceral, miserable,
vulnerable,
help me out of here.

keep me in this skin, it's all that shelters me
terrified, i testify that i
fever through every night.

chorus:
i never meant to build a life of blood
and bruise
everything i do is to walk my way,
to leave the weight,
become again,
someone new.

verse 2:
apathy stains all my words monotone,
tend to stay silent, re-wire my sirens,
hidden, they howl alone.

even unsteady we rise,
toughen up when tough luck cuts,
re-write the lines even with our wrists tied.

chorus:
i never meant to build a life of blood
and bruise
everything i do is to walk my way,
to leave the weight,
become again,
someone new.

bridge:
the clocks in my house keep ticking,
and talking to me,
my head's too loud, overcrowded,
and i can't breathe.

chorus:
i never meant to build a life of blood
and bruise
everything i do is to walk my way,
to leave the weight,
become again,
someone new.
let me be someone new.

conjugal visits, socks, and pens.

watching snow fall from the clenched fist of the sky
through slanted blinds,
from the window of a psych ward,
is an incredibly odd experience,
especially when you didn't know it could snow in texas.

it doesn't help when time stands still,
one clock in the entire facility,
stuck at 8:45.

from the first day,
i let the checkered floor become a chessboard.
build some sort of game
of all that would have been to hard to handle.

they called by number, not name,
(rp4765),
a bit like inmate
a bit like checkmate.

i am familiar with pawns.
have tried to pawn my life
for nothing in return,

for the first few days,

i wandered the hallways,
barefoot
with a sheet wrapped around my shoulders.

was baptized:
"the sarcastic one in a cape,"
the absolute best name i have ever been given.

to prove i could be trusted alone,
i played a lot of solitaire.
which is no easy feat,
with only thirty-eight cards (none of them aces).
i don't recollect winning a single game.

though group therapy was not mandatory,
i attended every session,
and was always on time
(8:45 am/pm).

most sessions consisted of playing bingo.
i won three times in a row,
was praised by the 'psychologist'
for my excellent critical thinking skills.

a group of us played uno one night,

and the same 'psychologist' walked around
and pulled cards from one person
and handed them to another player, at random.
to teach us what it means to adapt
to unexpected situations.

life is exactly like uno,
you just never know when a wild card
will be thrown your way,
which is to say,
medication is never the right decision,
since you can just adapt,
play the reverse card,
and everything will go away.

when i got out,
my father called and asked (in seriousness)
if i could please notify him in advance,
the next time i planned
on having a psychotic break.

i said yes, absolutely.
since i had learned that i just have to play
'skip your turn.'

a different psychologist told us:

"if you don't exercise you will be depressed forever."
so we started a petition for conjugal visits, titled
'sex-ercise and its benefits."
we got nearly everyone's signature.
it wasn't approved.
so instead, we wrote out a quick yelp resort review:

"the staff lacked a bit of knowledge
in the field of customer service.
especially when a guest,
that was meant to be in the homicidal ward,
sorry, had a room on a different hotel floor,
ran buck-naked down the hall
screaming david bowie lyrics, but backwards.
the concierge was not able to
catch him or ask him to please
let the other inmates, roommates; wait, sorry,
vacationers sleep."

after winning a game during one of our sessions,
i was rewarded with two pieces of candy.
i was able to find someone,
willing to take them in exchange for a pair of socks,
(she had an inside deal with one of the workers),
and kept a stash of socks hidden

rose devika.

under her mattress,
because the facility kept running out of
socks, jail pens, blankets,
medication,
and space (in the homicidal ward).

it's hard to be subtle
under constant fluorescent light,
but i was able to bargain
six pieces of paper torn from my journal
for a jail pen,
so i could write about
every crucial life lesson i had learned.

in seriousness,
i have never laughed as hard as i did
with some of the most resilient lunatics
i have ever met.

it is incredible,
how capable we are,
often unknowingly,
of making light of even
the darkest times in our lives.

the value of shock.

how awkward it has become
to be moved,
how quick we unhinge our mirrors,
lose our reflections,
searching for perfection
in silicone and plastic,
stretching the truth
like elastic.

how terrified we have become
of our own grief.
teeth tightening into barricade,
afraid of the weight we might swallow.

how hollow the contents of our conscience have become,
numbing ourselves,
into pre-programed reactions,
fractions
to calculate the right amount of time to grieve.

shift our thoughts into two-minute sympathy,
practice temporary empathy,
until another headline
finds its way to our timeline,

hands that know how to like,
not love.

amber alert,
insert scare tactic,
hyperactive,
quick trigger,
pull,
click,
gunshot.
how easily we digest obituary,
cemetery,
death,
death,
death.

rose devika.

bombing follows gunfire,
more barbed wire,
trump does dumb shit,
drunk driving incident,
affair investigation,
how easily we name
shock value worthy.

slow down,
don't let the muscle that is your heart atrophy,

do not let apathy govern your body.

there is a reason toll and poll sound alike,
the cost rises,
when we refuse to pay
attention.

crown valley parkway.

the gray car
flipped on its side,
like it was just laying down to rest.
wheels reaching,
slanted towards heaven.

like god,
with the flick of his forefinger,
decided to shift gravity
for just one fragment of a second.

the white jeep with the shattered windshield,
the bumper torn clean off.
its body, caving in,
maybe ran a red light,
maybe distracted,
maybe just a fraction of a second too quick,
maybe bad timing,
chalk it all up to bad luck,
chalk it all up to chance.

call it a stain,
something to be swept to the side of the road.
call it a life,
something to be swept under the rug.

i imagine
somebody on the other end of the road,
cursing the speed of traffic,
i imagine
somebody on the other end of the line,
clawing
at everything they thought they knew,
about the speed of life.

i imagine
somebody's someone
not coming home tonight.

when things fall apart,
they tend to do so in slow motion,
the reel, stuck on repeat.

rose devika.

and god,
just sitting there,
watching this terrible,
resilient world of ours spin
out of control,
slanted on its axis,

like a wheel
the moment before it loses its grip on the road.

sidewalks and where they take us.

i met her on a sidewalk somewhere
in new york city,
when she asked me for a lighter.

i was at my most reckless,
pushed her to the edge
of every one of her limits,
wanted her to leave,
but couldn't let go.

still stumbled
into slurred one-night stands,
didn't stand for anything,
and watched them fall for everything,
played cruel puppeteer.

i was only able to surrender to honesty,
was only able to loosen my grip on apathy
when she and i locked ourselves in the music room
for hours on end
the only thing that kept me from destruction.

the day we took the train to canada,
we dragged everything we owned
across the rain-soaked sidewalk.

they almost didn't let us cross the border,
because they thought we were running away.
we were running from everything.

the tsa agent read my journal,
i so far from an open book,
still a closed fist.

sometimes the story is beautiful,
but the circumstances cruel enough
to break every ounce of love.

we moved to california with all of our instruments,
and none of my will to live.
slept on two twin mattresses, side by side,
and fought about nothing at all,
all the time.

the day we moved to texas,
we found a free upright piano on the sidewalk.

moved it into our first ever apartment.

it was entirely out of tune,
but still in tune with itself.

somehow, we were the same.

after two years,
i finally said this has to be the end.
it had been for a long time.

after she moved out, we met again,
destroyed every part of the piano,
took hammers to its body, cut every string,
severed something.
took out two years of anger at the world
on our favorite fucked up piano,
still, some form of music.

the day she moved back to australia,
we said our goodbyes on the sidewalk.

i am sorry that the circumstances
never gave us a chance,
i am sorry i was never quite able to love you
the way you should have been loved.

but you were still the sweetest lesson in love,
in kindness,
in friendship.

sway.

verse 1:
turn the lights down low,
breathe me in, pull me close,
something sinister,
living in my head,
comfort me, resurrect,
'cause i know now,
that you can tame me
and talk me down.

chorus:
can't resist it,
do you crave this
we sway so slow
symmetry and jealousy,
are you watching me go
you're electric, mess me up.

verse 2:
walk across the wire,
somewhere between war and desire,
it's too still
and somber lately,
i need some heat, need you baby
'cause i know now

that you can tame me
and talk me down.

chorus:
can't resist it,
do you crave this
we sway so slow
symmetry and jealousy,
are you watching me go
you're electric, mess me up.

bridge:
bite your tongue, unravel me softly
i want to come undone.

chorus:
can't resist it,
do you crave this
we sway so slow
symmetry and jealousy,
are you watching me go
you're electric, mess me up.

conversation (in a hearse).

"i haven't seen you here before."

waiting for the mourning.

at night, my body becomes dead weight,
limbs turn into tombstones,
more paralysis, and less sleep.
every expiring breath, a eulogy,
for the things i have forgotten to remember.

all I can dig up are time capsule caskets.
the haunting, still unopened, dissociated ghosts,
induced amnesia.

i outline the bedsheets in chalk,
keep the crime scene quiet,
i have mastered the art of holding my breath,
and holding my silence.

and i may only be able to hold my breath for 46 seconds,
but i can hold my silence 7 years.

i play russian roulette with the contents of my conscience,
hypermnesia or repression,
mime or ruthless expression.

the skeletons in my closet keep begging to be cast,
in the leading role of this word play.

rose devika.

III.
oxygen
&
the lungs.

what i know about love i learned from living rooms (pt. 1).

bauji* wakes up at 6 am every morning,
tiptoes across the floorboards
and brings the nearly noiseless coffee machine
into the bathroom.
just to avoid waking us.

love, is the mattress he still keeps in storage,
the one we slept on for six months
on the living room floor
of his one-bedroom apartment.

bauji drinks a glass of red wine every night,
tells the same stories we have all heard so many times,
but never tire of,
every one of his laugh lines,
a story line I have memorized.

the story he tells most often is never about
my mother's mother, the one I never met,
or the woman he married after that, the one I considered
grandmother nearly all my life,

*bauji (बाउजी) is the punjabi word for maternal grandfather, or
'house elder.'

until she started exchanging shirtless photographs
with her high school boyfriend at 70 years old
via email.
then left for florida and hasn't been back since.

bauji says it took one hour to forgive
the affair
and I believe him.

because the story he tells most often,
is about the princess with whom he fell in love,
at 18 years old.
the one he bought a ring for,
but before he could ask,
her father married her off to an aristocrat,
because bauji was just a bollywood actor.
love is the fact that he has been telling this story
almost his entire life,
always with tears in his eyes,
but never a hint of bitterness.

love, is the magnet board on his fridge,
the one he keeps for grocery lists,
the one on which I wrote 'i love you,'

rose devika.

the month I moved in,
and it hasn't been erased since.

love, is the saran wrapped magnet board
he handed me a year later, after a visit,
the 'i love you' still untouched.
love is loving so much,
that you make space,
even when there is none.

copper

it has been over a year since i have written a poem.
maybe because i am too afraid of finding a truth,
that for once,
might not shift its shape on my tongue.

lately, my honesty runs out of breath
the moment my teeth unzip,
and I am far too quick at speaking the pacific ocean
into the shallow end of a swimming pool.

and though i have been trying to perfect my deep dive,
i just keep hitting rock bottom,
hoping to collect something worth keeping,
but i just keep coming up with copper.

i have enough pennies for every thought you own,
but i don't want to buy
into the belief that the truth is worth trading.

in middle school i put pennies on railroad tracks,
waited for the trains to flatten them,
so that i would have something to bring to show and tell,

and this feels a lot like that, like,
let me show you how well i can derail

every honest train of thought,

let me show you how many times
i have been dropped off at the same rock bottom station,
apparently to pick up pennies.

my pens keep running on empty,
so i have been casting out these lines,
hoping to hook into the dark side of my grief.
hoping to break bread over a table of contents,
i have yet to truly unfold.

i have been skipping coins across every wishing well,
waiting for something to finally bounce back,
waiting for the right way to write and tell,
but i just keep reeling in clichés, like, it hurts like hell.

like, most days nothing except that last line is true,
so I etch-a-sketch doctor my wounds,
lay my honesty on the surgical table,
make incisions where it has metastasized,
i resize,
fold its mass more manageable,
more digestible,
paint the picture pretty.
i am still the same guilty mortician.

rose devika.

so call this my polygraph machine mouth, call this unhinged,
or call this the first twitch of movement, regardless,
let me live fluent in telling the truth.
let me split open, become red sea.
there is still a war in the water,
there is still copper in this blood stream.

i am still diving to find the right depth.
i am still building a house of all the faulty wiring,
and though copper is a good conductor,
the orchestra of honest to god,
does not always follow directions well.

so let the music, the water, the war, swell,
let it build until the barricade breaks,
until the ache of never staying still,
becomes, again, familiarly foreign.

for now, i will keep all of this change.
until I can exchange it for a phone call,
somewhere in the middle of somewhere
where there is only a payphone,
so i can dial my history,
call my honesty and ask it to find its way home.

wherever that is, wherever that may be.

rose devika.

make light.

i will never say, "we were so young,"
because we had already lived lifetimes,
besides,
it was the oldest we'd ever been.

i will never say, "wisdom comes with age,"
we may have been far wiser then,
than we are now.

we used to climb trees in the canyon,
paint the palms of our hands
and trace our fingers
across wet cement,
youth,
and its relentless desire to leave a mark.

we used to climb up to that rooftop
smoke cigarettes and watch all the small
people,
and their pointlessness,
people,
and their infinite significance.

we used to drive far more miles
than we could afford,
the windows always down,
the sunroof always open,

we used to be made up of only motion,
just to find anywhere
where we could see
the city lights suspended beneath us.

we used to trust, fall
into each other,
read poems and suicide letters
wrote love letters and eulogies
in the backseat of the station wagon.

we used to spray paint reminders
and resolutions
in the hidden tunnels under fairview park,
where everything echoed endlessly.

rose devika.

when we walked in too deep,
darkness unlike any i have known
enveloped us entirely.
we dared each other to deprive all senses,
as long as we could,

then we would sprint towards that pinprick of light.

i don't know if any of us ever really found
the light at the end of the tunnel.
but we used to recklessly,
breathlessly, try to make light
of all that wasn't.
i used to press fingertips against fretboard
in 12th street park,
taught myself what it meant to find meaning,

played along to that symphony of wind,
still, we'd sing,
until we had memorized every song

of summer air and freedom,
however temporarily,
we got away from the cruelty we had come from.

we used to fuck and tell,
drink to feeling alive
on that empty stretch of beach,
we used to drink to death,
scream into the white of the waves,
until our lungs were empty enough,

to feel breath again,
and it always felt like it was the first.

rose devika.

write it down right.

verse 1:
this is my throne,
i rule cruel and alone
lived so many cities,
i still haven't walked my way back home
i fuck when i'm lonely,
i fight when i'm lost or in love,
incessant definitions,
i know i don't know very much, but

chorus:
sink your nails into my shoulder,
time capsule, capture the horror,
we'll save it for when we're older
'cause i need some grace
need to write it down right,
need to memorize
the look on your face
we could be saved.

verse 2:
this is the darkness,
it comes at a cost,
feel me falter,
the signals are off

i've got a knack for strings
and things that come undone
isn't it lovely
always being on the run
from something or someone, but

chorus:
sink your nails into my shoulder,
time capsule, capture the horror,
we'll save it for when we're older
'cause i need some grace
need to write it down right,
need to memorize
the look on your face
we could be saved.

bridge:
let the flood waters rise, capsize,
i'll be here,
shake in your sleep,
these lessons in fear
i'd still rather you stay.

rose devika.

chorus:
sink your nails into my shoulder,
time capsule, capture the horror,
we'll save it for when we're older
'cause i need some grace
need to write it down right,
need to memorize the look on your face
we could be saved.

something deafening tonight.

the leaves fall and flinch at the sharp lash,
of october's ruthless, restless wind,
something deafening tonight.

i run my fingertips across the braille
of all the bite marks we left
on each other's lips.

so cry.
swing your arms into flailing nooses,
until the air around you has rope burn.

throw your tantrums,
watch them boomerang back.
tonight, I cannot catch you.
there is no trust in the fall.

we have fallen in and out of love enough times,
we have driven across enough state lines,
to have read all the signs by now.

hafiz wrote, "i am trying the best i can
with this crude brush, the tongue,
to cover you with light."

tonight, I wrap only wrath around your shoulders,

let there be no light.
this tongue can be a brush or a knife.

and tonight, this body is not an instrument,
tonight, there is no more muse or music,
tonight, i am only blade,
trying to cut through tethered,
twisted heartstrings.

this, the end.
so let's let the curtains close.
let there be applause
for all the times we tried
and all the times we didn't.

rose devika.

like you do.

verse 1:
the wires got crossed,
what's love without loss
twist in your reigns,
call for a quick escape.

and we're both guilty,
of taking the easy way out
but i want it hard, want it rough,
leave me loud.

chorus:
take it all out on me,
your turn to listen,
my turn to speak.
i'll take it all out on you,
hazards and headlights, stop signs,
keep pushing through,
leave me like you do.

verse 2:
those cyanide eyes,
reflect the dark in mine
cold to the core,
leave all your skeletons at my door

and we're both cynical,
clinically looking for fire
language of touch, language of liars.

chorus:
take it all out on me,
your turn to listen,
my turn to speak.
i'll take it all out on you,
hazards and headlights, stop signs,
keep pushing through,
leave me like you do.

bridge:
i've got a tendency to be a little untamed,
and you've got a tendency to play childish games.

chorus:
take it all out on me,
your turn to listen,
my turn to speak.
i'll take it all out on you,
hazards and headlights, stop signs,
keep pushing through,
leave me like you do.

in some restaurant.

cheekbones cut out of marble.
etch-a-sketch people,
drawing and
re-drawing lives,
drawing and
re-drawing every fault line.
shake to erase every earthquake.

flickering candlelight reflects
off silver bracelets,
worth, neatly measured and cut,
wrapped around wrists, slender enough
to bend into submission with nothing but a word.

the man with the gold ring
traces his forefinger along the seam of her dress,
hand hovers over shoulder blade,
then waist,
pauses over zipper,
molds the clay into woman,
the woman into geometry.

she leans into him,
her face, the perfect poster
of a plastic surgeon's wet dream.

close to the bone.

verse 1:
see the tv static in your eyes,
see the gears twisting
as you say your goodbyes.
break down the walls of this glass house,
tell me that love
is a word you can't pronounce.

chorus:
tell me, is the devil alone tonight
is he burning up a fever
has he lost his fight.
tell me, do you have to cut so close to the bone,
do you like me lifeless
does it feel like home.

verse 2:
pace across the floor, keep your back straight,
crumble when you speak,
i'll carry your weight.
say everything you'll regret,
bend and break trust,
i'll learn to forget.

chorus:
tell me, is the devil alone tonight
is he burning up a fever
has he lost his fight.
tell me, do you have to cut so close to the bone,
do you like me lifeless
does it feel like home.

bridge:
tongue twist tragedy, dissonance and melancholy,
i'll let you down again.
speak to me honestly,
when you go leave my life softly,
let me down again.

chorus:
tell me, is the devil alone tonight
is he burning up a fever
has he lost his fight.
tell me, do you have to cut so close to the bone,
do you like me lifeless
does it feel like home.
like home.

what I know about love I learned from living rooms (pt. 2).

the first time i drove to that light blue
one-bedroom
back house,
after the car kept telling me to crash,
i finally unlatched all of my hinges,
let every door crack,
splinter,
my life an undone mosaic.

there was just enough rage and wreckage,
to finally unstitch 7 years of silence,
in the living room of my english teachers'
home,
where i learned that silence,
like fever,
has a breaking point.

that night she told me to come over anytime,
even if she wasn't home.
love, is the fact that she always offers tea,
or a place to sleep,
or to help carry my history,
in a place where there wasn't enough space.

love, is everything she continues to teach,
despite the fact that I have not been her student
for almost four years.

love, is the fact that she introduced me to writing,
drove two hours
to bring me to my first ever open mic
when i was 16 years old,
love, is every poem i practiced
in the middle of her dimly lit living room,

rose devika.

her unflinching honesty,
challenging me,
both tough and tender love.

love, is her telling me to tell
whatever needs to be told,
while telling me i cannot keep a constant hold
on the war,
there is no need to keep keeping it as a souvenir.

love, is the spare key she cut,
the one i often wear around my neck,
even from 1,441 miles away

a reminder that love,
has always
brought me back to safety,
found me somewhere to stay.

music is a muscle.

1.
i needed something to hold,
something curved enough to keep me
from writing only in right angles.
could only see the straight of my jaw
in the mirror,
tuned and tightened teeth.
could only speak in staccato,
taught enough to snap every arrow of string.
danger was everywhere.
fear, a loaded handgun.

2.
i found my mother's old
classical guitar in the garage,
after my first love left,
i played until my fingertips bled.

3.
when my mother's first love was killed at 18,
she spent months curled in the corner by the turntable,
chain-smoking,
and teaching herself guitar.

4.
once,
when she couldn't get out of bed, again,
jagged grief, clenched around every artery,
i laid the guitar in her arms.

her fingers, still knew the shaky melody.
music is muscle,
becomes memory so easily.

5.
the day I left,
my best friend gave me her 3/4 yamaha,
i could only afford one semester in new york,
spent my time drawing white lines,
writing white lies,
that hollow hallelujah,
the hollow of guitar.
learned to let that body of wood and body of mine
lean into one another,
comfort and raw rage.

6.
i tend to fight,
even when there's nothing to fight about,
we fought anyway.
broke up, made up, broke down.

7.
i don't remember the exact fight
i remember only that my ex-girlfriend gave me a fender
to prove that she believed in my artistry.
despite the lack of grounding,
i played that buzzing guitar incessantly,
through sobriety and apathy.

8.
i have small hands,
have a hard time with the bend,
the stretch it takes to reach the right note.

9.
i have never taken a lesson.
far too stubborn.

10.
the first guitar i ever bought was a used epiphone,
the strings, uncut,
when we played gigs,
i kept time with the rattle of strings.

11.
i was given a taylor for my 21st birthday
i am still terrified of touching it.

12.
i find chords based on images in my head.
cannot explain what i am doing or why,
music is a muscle,
knows the memory before i do.

the dark side of light.

verse 1:
they tend to like me most, the less they know
of the bricks i can build up around this glass house from which
i'm trying not to throw.
and yes, i'm so good at burning the bridges of my own feet,
but i learned resilience on the run, won't give my inner child custody.

chorus:
please don't let me break
back into a spine that bends to become
a bow that pulls heartstrings too tight
i'm tired of looking at the dark side of the light.
please let it be loud, drown out the voices,
i'm voiceless, they're violent, but most of them mine,
i invite them in for a drink, let's argue, let's overthink
the ruin is still better than the quiet.

verse 2:
i'm tall enough now to live the life they said i'd never reach,
the world is falling off its axis and i'm still falling for self-defeat.
and jesus christ, memory lane is a long road,
never leads to a driveway,
never leads to a home.

chorus:
please don't let me break
back into a spine that bends to become
a bow that pulls heartstrings too tight
i'm tired of looking at the dark side of the light.
please let it be loud, drown out the voices,
i'm voiceless, they're violent, but most of them mine,
i invite them in for a drink, let's argue, let's overthink
the ruin is still better than the quiet.

bridge:
and nothing's forever, so i'll go ahead
and sever every beautiful thing
it's dangerous to love something so much, inevitable hurt
so let me be the first to burn it down.

chorus:
please don't let me break
back into a spine that bends to become
a bow that pulls heartstrings too tight
i'm tired of looking at the dark side of the light.
please let it be loud, drown out the voices,
i'm voiceless, they're violent, but most of them mine,
i invite them in for a drink, let's argue, let's overthink
the ruin is still better than the quiet.

keeping track of grace.

track #1

tonight jeff buckley plays
on the record player.
slight scratch and static.

and there is nothing that moves me more.

it is said that buckley often wrote
and spoke about death,
both ironically,
and seriously.

someone recently said he sang
only songs of sadness,
knew nothing else.
the epitome of dark,
of brooding,
mystery.

jeff buckley once asked dave lory,
"do you ever, like, when you're on the highway,
and there's no one else around,
take your hands off the wheel?"

track #2

my favorite author, colum mccann,
writes every single one of his novels,
at a desk,
he has pushed into the dark of his closet.

he is often criticized about
the dark nature of his stories,
told he is incapable
of bringing to life,
a "happy book,"
one where the majority of his characters,
primarily the protagonists,
don't die.

rose devika.

track #3

all I will say about leonard cohen,
one of the most brilliant poets,
is that his last album,
the one right before his death,
was quite literally titled
'you want it darker.'

track #4

whenever apathy takes hold,
i listen to vivaldi's four seasons,
violin concerto no. 4 (winter)
in f minor,

only listen to dmitry sinkovsky's version,
because you can hear his breathing
through the entire piece,
something so riddled with emotion,
but still,
so rough around the edges.

track #5

i am often told it is crucial that i stop writing
such heavy pieces.

need to lighten the mood,
so that my readers
don't want to jump off a bridge,
before they've even gotten
through the acknowledgments.

i exclusively write in diners,
where the lights are always on.
drink enough coffee to keep me wired
the entire night.

so i locked myself in the closet last week,
with all the lights off.
thought maybe,
with just enough irony,
i could write a poem
filled with only happy.

rose devika.

to be clear,
i am not an unhappy person.
it is not the darkness
i am moved by most.

it is the resilience,
it is the grace,
both,
languages to learn.

it is how to turn every fracture,
every fragment,
into something
that might reach someone.

a letter.

i know you are already well aware of how deeply memory fascinates me. the way we remember. the way we are remembered. the things we keep ourselves from remembering. i know we both have a lot of blank pages between the table of contents and the acknowledgments. i know how subjective memory can be. how easily distorted. somehow, it seems to be both our link to the past and what keeps us chained to the present. i have arm wrestled with all of my past selves, argued over which one of us is correct so many times because it is nearly impossible not to project what i know now into what i didn't know then, when remembering, and that alone is enough to make the thought of trying to remember anything for what it really was seem futile. it feels like any life story becomes unreliable. so when i say i will remember you, it is not what i really mean.

i think the word 'remember' lacks something. it implies recalling.

memorizing is different. i wholeheartedly believe that it is the only way of capturing a moment or a person entirely and accurately. somehow, a way of suspending something in time that remains some form of infinite. and there is a conscious choice required to memorize, unlike remembering, which we do naturally.

like muscle memory, i honestly believe that the things i have memorized have become so much a part of me that they are built into my body.

i read about a man called clive wearing a while ago. he has both anterograde and retrograde amnesia. he remembers only that he has children and that he loves his wife. he is ecstatic to see her every single time, even if he saw her mere minutes ago. even time is taken when memory is lost. and i know that everything has an expiration date. i know that time is not on our side, which is why i intend to memorize all that we are, all that this is, to the best of my ability. and here's the thing about clive. he has no past. he has no future. but he can sit at his piano and play songs he learned decades ago absolutely flawlessly.

if i could, i would ask clive whether the emotion he once associated with a piece of music is a part of muscle memory,

rose devika.

too. and i know clive couldn't answer that. even if it was true, he would have no recollection. the same way he forgets he even played the piano a few moments after he stops playing.

still, i imagine that for one minuscule moment, his life becomes his life again. that he plays and feels all there is to feel again.

i have taught myself to play everything i know with my eyes closed for that exact reason. i have never written a single one of my chord progressions down. i want to know them all by heart or by muscle. that way i can play a song i wrote years ago, and the associated emotions become present, almost immediately.

reading 'patriotism' by yukio mishima had the same effect on me that the movie 'a ghost story' did. my reaction was so visceral it was jarring. both are stories that depict love, that depict life, that depict memory, that depict death. they both acted as catalysts for the phrase "memorize this" to repeat over and over in my head. mostly when i am with you.

all of that 'right now,' even after it has passed, is still present.

i have memorized the fabric of your sweater against my cheek,
the rough of rain-soaked concrete against bare feet,
the thrill of the way in which i hoped you might have been
watching me,
endlessness, even when it ends,
the softest part of you right above your collarbone
especially on the right side,
ash on the windowsill,
your laugh lines, but from a profile view,
i have memorized your story line and mine,
and their symmetry,
the rhythm of your breath changing in the church parking lot,
right next to the police station,
did you know that your hands were shaking, the first time you
traced across the outline of my jaw?
i have memorized every time our hands touched
before we knew that we both knew,
your hand against the floorboards,
your irises when you knew it was about you,
all of your tells,
the way your hands don't move when you tell me
that i am the last one you will ever love,
and love,
i know that is unlikely to be true,

rose devika.

but forever is now,
so i believe you.
i have memorized the poster on the window next to the parking
lot, where they turn tricks, and we just sit and talk and touch,
the way nostalgia sounds, changes the tone of your voice,
i have memorized the mirror of him you are terrified
of becoming,
the direction your feet face when you don't believe me, that
there is no chance in hell, you ever will.
the way you laugh, but don't like to,
what it feels like to love without boundary,
i have memorized the ridges of your shoulder blades
their rise and fall,
i have memorized how angry you are when you are angry at
yourself,
your nothing at all,
the words we should never have said,
the words we say that mean more than could be put into words,
which i know doesn't quite make sense,
i have memorized what it feels like to be loved, honestly.

it has become second nature.

i will never be able to translate what i have memorized onto paper, at least not in its entirety. but maybe that's the point. the trying. and what we get to keep to ourselves.

but if creating is the closest i can come to eternalizing all that i have memorized, if memorizing is the closest i can come to forever suspending moments that remain unchanged, even if everything else has changed, that is so much more than enough. what i think i mean to tell you is that i am positive that even if i forget how to remember, someday,
i will still have you memorized.

in muscle,
or maybe something more.

rose devika.

what I know about love I learned from living rooms (pt. 3).

in my first ever apartment,
there was a rusty nail that stuck out of the carpet,
i stepped on it almost every time i walked into the kitchen,
could never pull it loose.
three of the four burners were broken,
two of the two closet doors couldn't be opened,
without unhinging them entirely,
and the dishwasher hadn't washed dishes
since the 70's.

but love was walking through the living room,
the piano filled almost half of it,
the kitchen small enough to practically be a part of it.
it was the off-white refrigerator,
on it, the magnet board,
the 'i love you,' still untouched.

ACKNOWLEDGMENTS

thank you brian walker for the tremendous impact you have had on my life and artistry, for spending countless hours at the diner reading and editing every poem, and for your immeasurable kindness and generosity. thank you monika patterson for your infinite support, compassion, and for every moment we have been through together. thank you maddy monjo for believing in my work, for always pushing me to pursue what i love, and for all that we created together. thank you bauji (billy sharma), for teaching me so many lessons in love. thank you papaji, though we never met, for showing me what determination, resilience, and true passion look like. thank you renuka sharma for supporting my endeavors and for tattooing a line from one of my poems around your wrist. thank you robin theiss for your guidance, for introducing me to writing, and for reminding me of all there is to be grateful for. thank you lydia turino for every moment of youth. thank you tyler germaine for always being ready to take on any artistic endeavor at a moment's notice, for assisting with the photoshoot for this book, and for visually bringing these poems to life through videography. thank you amani sodiq, jordan dorsey, kyle bosarge, tyler germaine, and brian walker, for allowing me to photograph you. thank you julian aquin, chantelle jackson, melissa cornett, sabrina feldman, michaela kreim, gage kerley, sean poe, and nancy richard for your generosity and support. and thank you sebastian, for all that you are.

ABOUT THE AUTHOR

A consummate artist, yet an eternal seeker, Rose Devika offers poetry as a powerful reminder of authenticity, grit, and resilience. Winner of Say Word L.A.'s Youth Slam Competition, Rose joined a poetry team and toured Southern California at age 18. Committed to ambassadorship as a creator, Rose was a finalist for Youth Poet Laureate of both Los Angeles and New York City and facilitated weekly writing workshops for inmates at the Bronxville Correctional Facility.

A self-taught songwriter, singer, and musician, Rose formed and co-managed the band 'January Grit,' releasing their debut album 'Here in Fahrenheit' in January of 2019. Rose's debut solo full-length album is set for release in 2021.

Rose was born in Toronto, Canada and has since lived in several cities in Southern California and New York. She currently lives in Dallas, Texas with her dog, Luna.

Rose's music and poetry are available on all streaming platforms and can also be found on her website, www.rosedevika.org

CPSIA information can be obtained
at www.ICGtesting.com
Printed in the USA
FSHW021836200221
78695FS